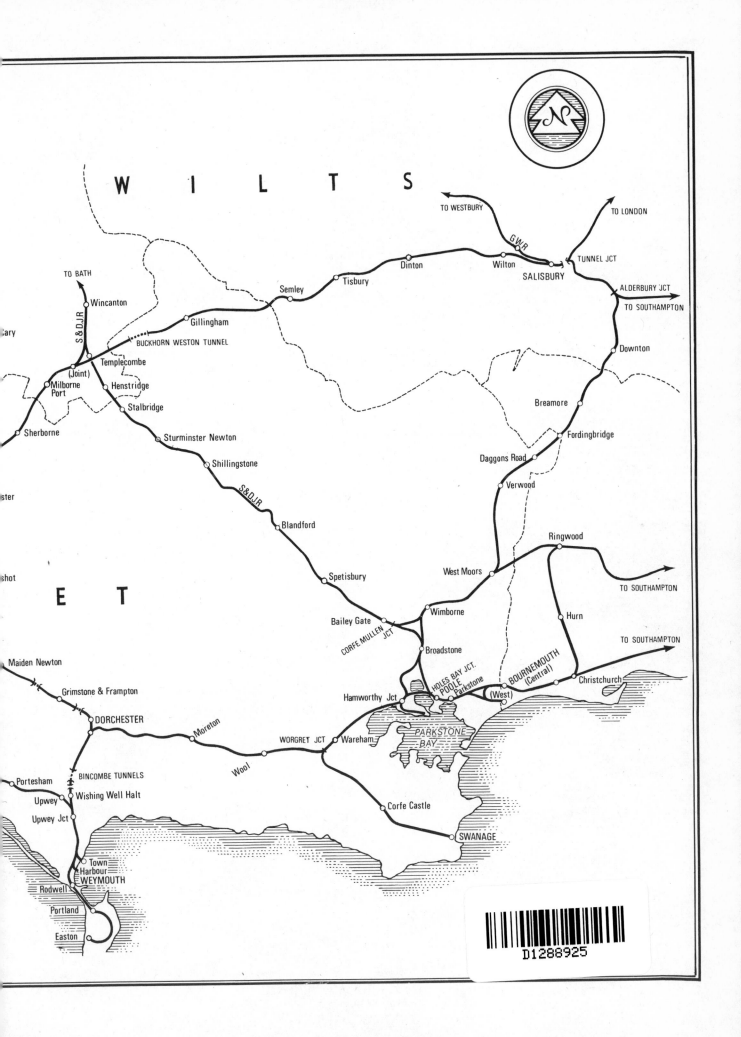

'Ivo Peters' SOUTHERN STEAM ALBUM

She was a phantom of delight
When first she gleamed upon my sight;
A lovely apparition, sent
To be a moment's ornament

William Wordsworth

Southern Elegance — *Belgian Marine*, one of the magnificent 'Merchant Navy' class Pacifics, climbs effortlessly towards Semley with an up West-of-England express.

Title page: 'Merchant Navy' Pacific No 35008 *Orient Line* approaches Bournemouth Central with the 10.08am Bournemouth West-Waterloo.

'Ivo Peters'
SOUTHERN
STEAM ALBUM

LONDON

IAN ALLAN LTD

First published 1979

ISBN 0 7110 0912 0

Published by Ian Allan Ltd, Shepperton, Surrey;
and printed in the United Kingdom by
Ian Allan Printing Ltd

Introduction

The old London and South Western main line from Salisbury to Exeter, brilliantly planned and superbly built, was a magnificent piece of railway engineering.

From Salisbury the line runs westwards in a series of sweeping undulations. Long down-hill stretches are followed by banks of increasing length and severity as the railway progresses through the beautiful, rolling countryside of first Wiltshire, then briefly Dorset and Somerset, and finally Devonshire.

So superb is the alignment that in the days of steam, once Wilton had been passed, there were no speed restrictions, and drivers would come tearing downhill to get up as much impetus as possible for the attack on the bank which lay ahead. This made for a thrilling ride, for with no limit placed on downhill running, speeds of 80mph and over at the bottom of the 'dips' were commonplace.

Today the scenery throughout the run from Salisbury to Exeter is still as beautiful as ever, but sadly this once splendid main line is now but a shadow of its former self, having been singled in 1967, and reduced to near impotence.

The pictures in this book have been arranged in 'journey

order'. First we travel west from Salisbury to Exeter (Plates 1-138), with a brief detour down the Yeovil-Dorchester line and looking in on the Axminster-Lyme Regis, and Seaton Junction-Seaton branches on the way.

The second part of the book is devoted to the line from Bournemouth to Weymouth (Plates 139-211), including a run up to Broadstone, and some pictures on the Swanage branch.

A map of the lines covered, together with the gradient profiles, will be found in the endpapers of the book.

Acknowledgements

I am most grateful to Lawrence Popplewell, George Pryer and Peter Smith for giving me information which has been of great help when preparing the captions for the pictures in this book.

My old friend Peter Smith — one-time engineman on the Somerset and Dorset — also very kindly checked through my manuscript, and so saved me from committing several bloomers!

I would also like to record my warm thanks to Peggy Leitch for once again taking on the task of deciphering my illegible handwriting and typing my manuscript. And last, but not least, a very sincere 'thank you' to the three people who through their constructive criticism are always of immense help to me in the preparation of my books — my sister Luise Girdlestone, the Rev John Brennan and Angela O'Shea.

Ivo Peters

Part One
Salisbury to Exeter

1 *Above:* Two BR Standard 2-6-4 tanks, Nos 80152 and 80016, hauling an enthusiasts' special, turn south east at Tunnel Junction for the run from Salisbury down to Eastleigh on 17 September 1966.

Tunnel Junction Salisbury

Tunnel Junction lies on the north eastern outskirts of Salisbury. Immediately on emerging from Fisherton Tunnel, a line diverges from the Salisbury-Waterloo main line to run south east for Southampton and Portsmouth.

Up to 1964 there used to be a junction on this line at Alderbury, where trains could turn south west to run down through Fordingbridge to join the Broadstone-Brockenhurst line at West Moors.

2 *Right:* BR Class 5 No 73162 starts to gather speed as she passes Tunnel Junction on 4 July 1964 with the 12.06pm Salisbury to Waterloo.

3 *Below:* After making a cautious exit from Fisherton Tunnel, the driver of M7 0-4-4T No 30108 — in charge of another enthusiasts' special — opens the regulator as his train diverges from the main line to head off down towards Romsey on 23 March 1963.

Salisbury

The Southern Railway and Great Western Railway stations at Salisbury were situated side by side.

The first Great Western train to arrive in Salisbury was in 1856, the company's broad gauge Westbury-Warminster branch having been extended on a further 19½ miles to reach the city in June of that year. At that time the London and South Western Railway's line from Bishopstoke (Eastleigh) terminated at Milford, a mile away from the GWR terminus on the other side of the city. However, when the L&SWR Basingstoke-Andover line was extended to Salisbury, a new station was built alongside the GWR terminus and opened on 1 May 1857.

4 *Above:* 'Battle of Britain' class Pacific No 34072 *257 Squadron* standing at the west end of the station, and waiting for the road, with an express from Brighton to Plymouth. This through working was a regular turn for Bulleid 'WC' and 'BB' Pacifics in their original condition. Initially, weight restrictions west of Exeter precluded the use of these engines in their rebuilt form, but this embargo was lifted in 1959.

5 *Above:* Rebuilt 'BB' Pacific No 34056 *Croydon*, in charge of an up West-of-England express, running in past the GWR signalbox at the western end of the station on 29 September 1962.

6 *Below:* 'Merchant Navy' Pacific No 35014 *Nederland Line* comes in carefully round the sharp curve at the east end of the station with the down 'Atlantic Coast Express'.

Although of modern appearance, the East Box, on the right hand side of the picture, was built by the L&SWR in 1902. The 'new look' came in 1928 when the signalling equipment was being modernised, and at the same time the old hip roof was replaced by a flat one made of concrete. As a matter of interest, this was the year when the East Box became 'Electro-pneumatic', but a similar plan for the West Box was never carried out.

Salisbury

In 1958 the British Transport Commission arranged a mobile 'Transport Treasures' exhibition which toured the country. Two bogie vehicles were adapted for the display of the many fascinating exhibits, and also on view was the preserved Midland-Glasgow & South Western Joint Stock twelve-wheeled dining car. When the Transport Treasures visited Salisbury at the beginning of March, a most interesting added attraction was the display of the preserved L&SWR Adams 4-4-0 No 563 which was placed at the head of the exhibition train.

7 *Above:* For the display at Salisbury, the exhibition vehicles were positioned in the down bay platform at the west end of the station. At the head of the train stands the preserved L&SWR Adams 4-4-0 No 563, whilst on the main line, BR Standard Class 5 4-6-0 No 73111 sets off with a stopping train for Yeovil Junction.

8 *Below* and **10** *Below right:* No 563 was designed by William Adams and built at Nine Elms in 1893. This engine, most beautifully restored in L&SWR livery, is now on display at the National Railway Museum, York.

9 *Right:* 'King Arthur' class 4-6-0 No 30451 *Sir Lamorak* drifts slowly past the Adams 4-4-0 as she sets back to pick up a luggage van.

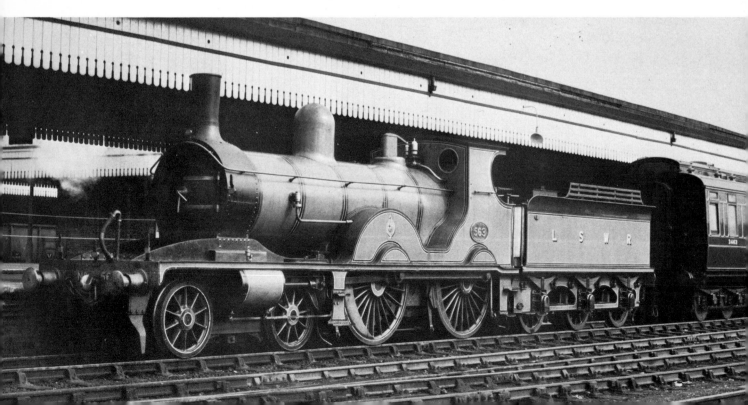

11 *Left:* M7 0-4-4T No 30033, on station pilot duties, comes carefully round the sharp curve at the east end of the station.

12 *Below:* S15 class 4-6-0 No 30835, in charge of a down goods, stands in the station, waiting for the road on 21 March 1964.

Salisbury

At the beginning of the century, trans-Atlantic liners from America were calling in at Plymouth to disembark passengers and mail. This traffic was then taken on to London by the London & South Western Railway and the Great Western Railway, the L&SWR conveying the passengers and the GWR the mail. Intense rivalry built up between the two companies to see whose train could reach London first, and tragically this ended in a dreadful catastrophe at Salisbury. In the early hours of 1 July 1906, the L&SWR driver attempted to take the sharp curve just to the east of the station at an impossible speed, resulting in the most horrific accident. One outcome of this tragedy was that from then on, nearly all trains were scheduled to stop at Salisbury, and for those that did run through, a severe speed restriction was imposed of 10mph, applicable between the East and West signalboxes.

13 *Above: Ellerman Lines*, one of the rebuilt 'Merchant Navy' class Pacifics, makes an impressive departure from Salisbury with the down 'Atlantic Coast Express on 28 October 1961.

14 *Right:* Travelling on the footplate on this occasion was Air Commodore C. M. Wight-Boycott, CBE, DSO RAF, the then Commandant of the Royal Observer Corps. (A pity the engine could not have been the 'Battle of Britain' class Pacific No 34050 *Royal Observer Corps.*

Salisbury
Motive Power Depôt

15 *Above:* An assortment of motive power lined up outside Salisbury shed on 23 March 1958. From the left, the locomotives are — BR Class 5 4-6-0 No 73114, U class 2-6-0 No 31614, T9 4-4-0 No 30301, an unidentified BR Class 4, U class 2-6-0 No 31804, a GWR 2-6-0, BR Class 4 4-6-0 No 75077, and S15 4-6-0 No 30829.

16 *Below:* Salisbury Coaling Stage. U class 2-6-0 No 31804 is being coaled, whilst N15 4-6-0 No 30454 *Queen Guinevere* waits her turn.

17 *Right:* S15 4-6-0 No 30829. This was one of a batch introduced by Maunsell in 1927. These engines differed from the original Urie design in certain respects, including having a higher boiler pressure, $\frac{1}{2}$in off the cylinder diameter, and a smaller grate. Externally they could be recognised from the original Urie engines by their modified cab and running plate.

18 *Left:* Rebuilt 'Merchant Navy' Pacific No 35009 *Shaw Savill*.

19 *Below:* H15 4-6-0 No 30522 and U 2-6-0 No 31804.

Salisbury
Motive Power Depôt

20 *Above:* Two BR Standard Class 4 2-6-4 tanks on Salisbury Shed on 17 September 1966. The engines had brought in an enthusiasts' special from the east, and were visiting the shed for turning and servicing before working the train down to Eastleigh. (See Plate 1).

21 *Below:* Bulleid 'West Country' and 'Battle of Britain' Pacifics face to face on Salisbury shed — No 34099 *Lynmouth* and No 34054 *Lord Beaverbrook*.

22 *Above:* One of Drummond's excellent T9 4-4-0s, No 30301 standing ahead of '700' class 0-6-0 No 30698 and U class 2-6-0 No 31614. No 30301 was one of a batch of T9s introduced in 1900. These engines differed from the original design in having wider cabs and splashers, and no coupling rod splashers. (See Plates 72 and 176).

23 *Below:* Dignity and impudence! One of the little Beattie 2-4-0 well-tanks, No 30587, built in 1874, stands alongside the massive bulk of BR 9F 2-10-0 No 92231, built 84 years later, in 1958. No 30587 was on her way from her home shed in Cornwall, to Eastleigh Works.

Nearing Wilton

For the first 2½ miles westwards from Salisbury, the Southern and Great Western lines ran side by side. Then shortly before reaching Wilton station, the Southern curves sharply to the south west, whilst the former GWR line veers away to the north west to head off towards Warminster and Westbury. The SR and GWR had their own separate stations at Wilton.

In 1973 a connection was put in between the two lines to the east of Wilton station, and today all trains use the Southern line between Wilton and Salisbury.

24 *Left:* BR Class 5 No 73166, in charge of the 11.58am (SO) Bideford to Waterloo, sweeps round the curve east of Wilton station to join company with the GWR for the final 2½ miles into Salisbury.

25 *Below:* The 2.00pm (SO) Ilfracombe to Waterloo, hauled by No 34010 *Sidmouth*, heads east from Wilton in the late afternoon of 10 August 1963.

26 *Above:* On 4 July 1964, No 34030 *Watersmeet*, runs leisurely towards Wilton with the 3.05pm down stopping train from Salisbury to Exeter.

27 *Below:* In bright evening sunshine, 'Battle of Britain' Pacific No 34070 *Manston*, coasts in towards Wilton with the 3.35pm down semi-fast from Waterloo to Yeovil.

Wilton

28 *Above:* Just to the east of Wilton station, a road bridge spanning both the Southern and Great Western lines, made a wonderful 'grandstand' from which to watch the trains. In this composite picture — the two photographs were taken within five minutes of each other on 27 July 1963, — the Southern train is the 9.10am (SO) Littleham to Waterloo, hauled by No 34070 *Manston* . . .

29 *Left:* The typical L&SWR style signalbox at Wilton was situated at the east end of the up platform. Passing through the station on a hot morning in August 1963, is rebuilt 'West Country' Pacific No 34003 *Plymouth* in charge of the 10.30am (SO) Ilfracombe to Waterloo.

30 *Right:* An immaculate 'Merchant Navy', No 35017 *Belgian Marine*, passes through the station with a Stephenson Locomotive Society Special bound for Exeter.

. . . whilst the Great Western train, drawn by an unidentified 'Hall', is the 9.06am (SO) Cardiff to Portsmouth.

Wilton

An attractive feature at Wilton was the signals. Because of the sharp curve through the station, the arms were mounted on tall L&SWR type lattice posts for easier sighting. The Up and Down Starters also carried a repeater arm mounted lower down the post in a position more easily observed by drivers of trains which had stopped in the station. The lower arm — called a 'Co-acting' arm — worked in unison with the upper arm, both being operated by the same lever in the signalbox.

31 *Above:* With the demise of the N15 'King Arthur' class, the 20 BR Standard Class 5 4-6-0s allotted to the Southern Region were given names previously carried by N15s. On 27 July 1963, one of these named Class 5s, No 73086 *The Green Knight* — with the regulator closed, but still travelling pretty fast — came sweeping through the station with the 9.10am (SO) Torrington to Waterloo.

32 *Left:* 'Battle of Britain' class Pacific No 34074 *46 Squadron*, running in with an up local on 29 September 1962.

Eastern Invasions!

33 *Above:* Ex-LNER Gresley A4 Pacific No 60024 *Kingfisher* passing through the station on 27 March 1966, with the Locomotive Club of Great Britain's 'A4 Commemorative Rail Tour'.

34 *Below:* Later in the same year, the LCGB organised another special over the Southern West-of-England main line, hauled by an Eastern Region Pacific. On this occasion, 14 August, the locomotive was a Peppercorn A2 class, No 60532 *Blue Peter*. Happily, *Blue Peter* has been preserved. Although, strictly speaking, not an ex-LNER engine — having been completed some three months after the railways of Britain had been nationalised — *Blue Peter* has been beautifully restored in LNER livery.

West of Tisbury

From Wilton the railway runs westwards up the valley of the river Nadder through some of the most beautiful countryside in Wessex. Over these 15 miles the tendency is for the line to be climbing steadily all the way to Semley, the final two miles being at 1 in 145.

35 *Above:* No 35008 *Orient Line*, coming downhill at high speed towards Tisbury with an up West-of-England express on 2 May 1950. In this picture, No 35008 is in her original condition: rebuilding of the 'Merchant Navys' did not commence until 1956.

36 *Below:* In late afternoon sunshine, No 35009 *Shaw Savill* climbs steadily westwards from Tisbury with the 3pm (SO) Waterloo to Ilfracombe on 27 July 1963.

Nearing Semley

37 *Above:* No 35013 *Blue Funnel*, tackling vigorously the last two miles of 1 in 145 up to Semley with the 4pm (Sundays) Waterloo to Exeter, on 27 August 1961. No 35013 was the third 'Merchant Navy' to be modified, rebuilding being completed in May 1956.

38 *Below:* On a beautiful summer's day fragrant with the scent of new-mown hay, S15 No 30844 draws near to Semley with the 3.05pm down local from Salisbury.

Semley

Semley marks the end of the 15 mile climb from Wilton. Just beyond where the station used to be, the line passes beneath the Warminster–Shaftesbury main road, and then sweeps down hill for 4 miles at 1 in 100 and 1 in 130, to Gillingham.

In years gone by, considerable milk traffic was handled at Semley, a milk factory situated alongside the line being served by a siding on the up side at the west end of the station.

39 *Left:* 9 August 1958. An up local from Yeovil arrives, double-headed by U class 2-6-0 No 31793 and N class 2-6-0 No 31414.

40 *Below:* — At Semley, the U came off to remain behind to shunt milk tank wagons, whilst the N set off for Salisbury with the local.

41 *Above:* On a miserable day in March 1964, and with the first spatters of rain just starting to fall, No 34096 *Trevone*, sets off into the gloom with an up local.

42 *Below:* The 1.14pm down stopping train from Salisbury runs in, drawn by S15 4-6-0 No 30827.

Between Semley and Buckhorn Weston Tunnel

From Semley the line descends for 4 miles at 1 in 100 and 1 in 130 down to Gillingham, before commencing to climb again at 1 in 300, and finally 1 in 100, up to the east end of Buckhorn Weston Tunnel.

43 *Above:* 'Battle of Britain' Pacific No 34078 *222 Squadron*, in immaculate condition, climbing uphill from Gillingham with the 10.15am (SO) Waterloo to Bideford.

44 *Below:* No 30453 *King Arthur* making an excellent climb up the final stretch of 1 in 100 towards Semley with the 11.45am (SO) Bude to Waterloo on 9 August 1958.

45 *Above:* On a sunny day in early autumn 1959, S15 No 30832, in charge of a short westbound goods, nears Buckhorn Weston Tunnel and the end of the climb from Gillingham.

46 *Below:* The 11am Plymouth to Brighton, hauled by 'Battle of Britain' Pacific No 34061 *73 Squadron*, running downhill towards Gillingham on 27 June, 1964.

Buckhorn Weston Tunnel

The summit of the 2¼ mile climb from Gillingham lies just to the east of Buckhorn Weston Tunnel. Through the 742 yard-long tunnel the line descends westwards at 1 in 100, and then continues to sweep on downhill at 1 in 100 and 1 in 90 for a further two miles before levelling out and commencing to climb steeply once again.

47 *Above:* Leaving the tunnel on 2 September 1961, is the 9.10am (SO) Torrington to Waterloo, drawn by No 34108 *Wincanton.*

48 *Below:* No 34024 *Tamar Valley* climbs up out of the tunnel with the 9.38am (SO) Littleham to Waterloo on 16 August 1958.

49 *Above:* The 6am Plymouth to Waterloo hauled by 'West Country' Pacific No 34015 *Exmouth*, heads away from Buckhorn Weston Tunnel on 27 June 1964.

50 *Below:* The down 'Atlantic Coast Express', hauled by 'Merchant Navy' Pacific No 35028 *Clan Line*, approaching Buckhorn Weston Tunnel on 2 September 1961. *Clan Line* is one of the Bulleid Pacifics which has been preserved. The Merchant Navy Preservation Society has made a magnificent job of the restoration of this locomotive which is maintained in absolutely splendid condition.

Buckhorn Weston Tunnel

51 *Left:* No 34096 *Trevone* emerging from Buckhorn Weston Tunnel with the 8.25am Plymouth to Waterloo on 15 August 1964.

52 *Below:* The 12.16pm up local ex-Templecombe emerges from the tunnel on 16 August 1958, hauled by S15 No 30841. This is another Southern engine which has been preserved. Restored in SR green livery and given the name *Greene King*, No 841 is now running on the North Yorkshire Moors Railway.

The crossover — partially dismantled — in the foreground was installed in March 1958 in connection with the relining of the tunnel, a job that made single line working necessary. Each line was used in turn for the running of traffic whilst the other was occupied by the Engineer's Department. A temporary signalbox, called Abbey Ford and opened on 9 March, was provided to work the singled section of line. The box was then closed from 2 April when single line working ceased for the duration of the heavy summer traffic, re-opening again on 21 September for the completion of the work.

53 *Right:* No 35011 *General Steam Navigation* and her heavy up West-of-England express caught 'bending' over the summit on a summer's morning in 1959.

54 *Below right:* 'Merchant Navy' Pacific No 35023 comes tearing down towards the tunnel at high speed with an excursion special in June 1966.

Templecombe

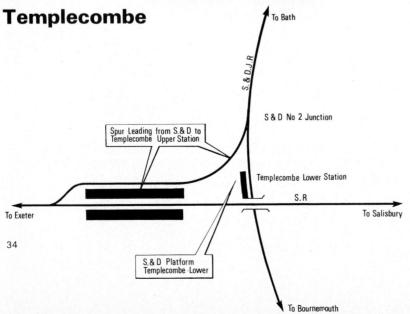

To Bath

S.&D.J.R

S & D No 2 Junction

Spur Leading from S.& D to
Templecombe Upper Station

Templecombe Lower Station

S.R

To Exeter

To Salisbury

S.& D Platform
Templecombe·Lower

To Bournemouth

55 *Above:* Just to the east of Templecombe station, the Southern crossed over the Somerset & Dorset line from Bath to Bournemouth — sadly now but a memory, for nothing remains today of this once splendid railway.

Somerset & Dorset trains calling at Templecombe, used the outer face of the up platform of the SR station. Just how they managed to carry out this complicated manoeuvre, is explained in my book *The Somerset & Dorset — an English Cross-Country Railway*. The S&D also had — but very rarely used — a 'station' of their own at Templecombe. This consisted of a short platform on the up side of the line, just north of where it passed underneath the Southern. In S&D timetables, their platform was referred to as 'Templecombe Lower' and the SR station as 'Templecombe Upper'.

In this picture, taken on 9 July 1955, T9 4-4-0 No 30721 has just set off from Templecombe with an up local, and is passing over the S&D line, on the right of which is 'Templecombe Lower' platform.

56 *Above:* A down Somerset & Dorset train, which had called at Templecombe Upper, is drawn out backwards and down the spur by Z class 0-8-0T No 30953. Once the Z had hauled the engine clear of S&D No 2 Junction, she would be uncoupled, and the S&D engine, which had remained attached at the head of the train throughout, would then set off south again for Bournemouth.

57 *Below:* Stanier 'Black Five' No 45493 and 'West Country' Pacific No 34100 *Appledore*, emerge from the deep cutting west of Templecombe with a special excursion train organised by the Locomotive Club of Great Britain.

Milborne Port

The steep climb through Templecombe, much of it at 1 in 100 and 1 in 80, ends a little to the east of Milborne Port. For the next nine miles, apart from a brief up grade near Wyke, the line is now level or falling all the way to Yeovil Junction. In the days of steam, this was fine if you were travelling west, but for eastbound trains, those nine miles were a long, hard slog.

58 *Above:* With the shadows beginning to lengthen on a cold autumnal evening in October 1963, No 35018 *British India Line* and her eastbound express are caught by the rays of the setting sun as they climb towards Milborne Port.

59 *Below:* After less than a mile of downhill running, speed was already beginning to build up as 'Battle of Britain' Pacific No 34088 *213 Squadron* came swiftly through Milborne Port one evening in early October 1963, heading into the westering sun with her down express.

60 *Right:* U class 2-6-0 No 31622 passes Milborne Port Up Distant signal as she gallops gaily westwards with the 3.34pm Templecombe to Exeter on 1 August 1960.

61 *Below right:* On an overcast and oppressive day in late summer 1964, BR Standard Class 4 2-6-0 No 76007 in charge of an eastbound freight, toils wearily up a long stretch of 1 in 80 towards Milborne Port.

Between Milborne Port and Sherborne

62 *Above:* A sullen and depressing day of drenching rain in July 1964, had matured into a vivid, fragrant summer's evening as No 34001 *Exeter* came pounding up the bank from Sherborne with an up West-of-England express.

63 *Left:* The 1pm Waterloo to Plymouth, hauled by 'Merchant Navy' Pacific No 35006 *Peninsular & Oriental SN Co*, travelling very fast downhill from Milborne Port towards Sherborne on 1 August 1964.

A Contrast in Loads
for *Croydon!*

64 *Above:* On 15 August 1964, 'Battle of Britain' Pacific No 34056 *Croydon* ambles up the long bank from Sherborne towards Milborne Port with the one-coach 5.05pm local from Yeovil Junction to Templecombe . . .

65 *Below:* . . . but a week later, on 22 August 1964 *Croydon* found herself faced with a very different proposition! This time she was in charge of the very heavy Okehampton-Surbiton car ferry — and *Croydon* sounded superb as she fought her way up the long stretch of 1 in 80 towards Milborne Port.

Between Milborne Port and Sherborne

66 *Above:* The 2.56pm Yeovil to Salisbury heading east from Sherborne, hauled by 'West Country' Pacific No 34008 *Padstow.*

67 *Below:* By 1964, many of the local services previously handled by the mixed traffic S15 4-6-0s, had been taken over by BR Standard Class 4 4-6-0s. On 18 July 1964 BR Class 4 No 75005 drops downhill towards Sherborne with the two-coach 5.34pm Templecombe to Yeovil.

68 *Left:* On a bitterly cold winter's morning, N class 2-6-0 No 31846 labours slowly up the long bank towards Milborne Port with a heavy eastbound goods.

Eastbound Freight

69 *Right:* 'Merchant Navy' Pacific No 35023 *Holland-Afrika Line* passing under a farm bridge east of Sherborne with an up freight on a beautiful, still, autumn day in October 1963.

Sherborne

70 *Left:* Sherborne lies four miles west down the bank from Milborne Port. In the days of steam, with a mile of the descent as steep as 1 in 80, westbound expresses would be travelling at high speed as they came into view round the bend to the east of the station: it was an exciting spectacle, not easily forgotten.

Early in the evening of 8 August 1964, No 34093 *Saunton* must have been well up into the 80s as she flashed over the level crossing just to the east of the station with a down West-of-England express.

Sherborne's modern-style signalbox, opened on 18 December 1960, replaced the original L&SWR box which had been situated on the down side of the line, immediately opposite the new box.

71 *Below:* In the spring of 1953 the Southern Region ran into serious trouble with their 'Merchant Navy' Pacifics. The entire class had to be withdrawn from service for examination, and to tide matters over, several locomotives were borrowed from other Regions. (See Plates 99 and 100).

In this picture taken on 23 May 1953, 'Britannia' Pacific No 70017 *Arrow*, on loan to Salisbury Shed from Old Oak Common MPD, Western Region, is tackling well the climb east from Sherborne with the 2.30pm Exeter to Waterloo.

East of Yeovil Junction

72 *Above:* T9 4-4-0 No 30718 drawing near to Yeovil Junction on 14 August 1960, with a special excursion organised by the Railway Correspondence & Travel Society.

73 *Left:* The Sunday 11.48am Yeovil to Salisbury, hauled by S15 4-6-0 No 30831, heading east from Yeovil towards Sherborne.

The original S15 design was by R. W. Urie for the L&SWR in 1920. After the Grouping, further engines of this class were constructed by Maunsell, who had modified the design in certain respects. No 30831 was one of a batch introduced in 1927.

Yeovil Junction

74 *Above:* On a bright November Sunday morning in 1963, 'Battle of Britain' Pacific No 34063 *229 Squadron* makes a brisk departure from Yeovil Junction with the 11.50am for Salisbury.

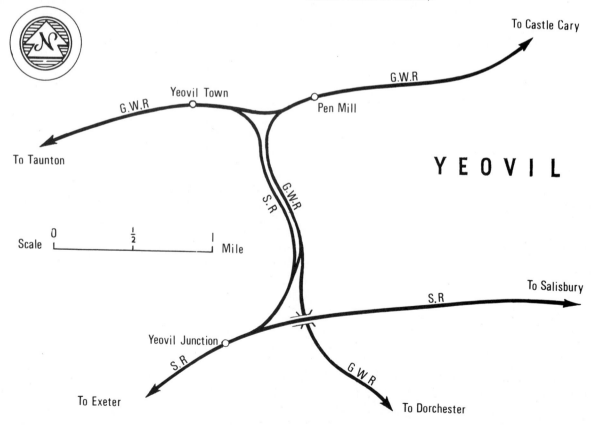

75 *Top:* After being held for a while at the east end of the station, S15 No 30845 gets the road, and sets off again with her up goods into the growing gloom of a dull October afternoon in 1962.

This picture shows a typical example of a Southern gantry signal. The arms read (left to right) Bay to Branch, Bay to Main, Up Local to Branch, Up Local to Main (off), Up Through to Branch, Up Through to Main. The Banner repeater on the end, of which this is a rear view, repeated Yeovil Junction 'B' Box Down Through Home.

76 *Above:* Early in 1965, a sudden but temporary shortage of DMUs in the West Country, led to two small ex-Great Western 0-4-2 tanks being hastily borrowed from Yeovil shed in order to work the Seaton branch for a short while. Coupled together, Nos 1442 and 1450 travelled west down the main line from Yeovil to Exmouth Junction shed on Sunday, 7 February. At the start of their journey, the engines were running bunker-first, so a brief halt was made to use the turntable at Yeovil Junction. Both engines were turned together — quite a rare sight! (See also Plates 106 and 125).

Yeovil Town

77 *Above:* A frequent local service was run between Yeovil Town, Yeovil Junction and Yeovil, Pen Mill. This normally consisted of two coaches worked by an M7 0-4-4T, the engine hauling the train from Yeovil Junction to Yeovil Town and from Pen Mill to Yeovil Town, and propelling on the return runs. In this picture, M7 No 30129 and her two coaches are standing at the western end of Yeovil Town station. Before nationalisation, this was a joint station shared by the GWR and SR. The signals were an assortment of the two companies; but the signalbox was pure Great Western.

78 *Below:* M7 No 30131 propels her train into the station on 14 August 1960. On the right in this picture is Yeovil shed, which was situated just to the south of the station.

Yeovil Town Station 5 August 1962

79 *Above:* 'West Country' Pacific No 34007 *Wadebridge* draws forward after bringing in an up stopping train from Exeter. On shed on the right is N class 2-6-0 No 31810. The two signals in this picture are both ex-Great Western lower quadrant.

80 *Below:* M7 No 30129 stands in the station with her two coaches which she was about to propel to Pen Mill. On the right, N class 2-6-0 No 31810 is engaged in shunting stock.

81 *Bottom:* A picture taken a few minutes later at the eastern end of the station. M7 No 30129 has just set off, propelling her two coaches to Pen Mill, whilst standing in the station, waiting for the road, is ex-GWR pannier tank No 8745 with a two-coach local to Yeovil Junction. The Starting signal is an SR upper quadrant.

Yeovil Town–Pen Mill

The line connecting Yeovil Town with Pen Mill was $\frac{1}{2}$ mile long and single track. The setting was extremely attractive, the line curving round beneath a steep hill, and being bordered on both sides by tall stately trees.

82 *Above:* Drummond M7 0-4-4T. No 30131 sets off from Yeovil Town in the early afternoon of 14 August 1960, propelling her train towards Pen Mill. The line curving round to the right ran to Yeovil Junction.

83 *Left:* A little later in the afternoon, No 30131 appeared again through the trees, heading back towards Yeovil Town with a return working from Pen Mill.

Between Yeovil Town and Yeovil Junction

The line from Yeovil Town to Yeovil Junction was double track and just under two miles long. Setting off from Yeovil Town, the railway curved round towards the south and was soon joined by the GWR Castle Cary-Weymouth line. The two lines then ran parallel for a mile before the Southern turned south west to run into Yeovil Junction, whilst the Great Western headed on south, to pass beneath the Southern Salisbury-Exeter main line ½ mile east of Yeovil Junction.

84 *Above:* By 1963, small ex-Great Western 0-4-2 tanks had started to take a hand in working the local shuttle service between Yeovil Town, Yeovil Junction and Pen Mill. In the fleeting sunshine of a cold afternoon in late autumn 1963, ex-GWR 0-4-2T No 1442 heads back towards Yeovil Town with her two-coach train from Yeovil Junction.

85 *Below:* On a hot sultry afternoon in high summer 1962, Drummond M7 0-4-4T No 30129 passes by, propelling her train from Yeovil Town towards Yeovil Junction.

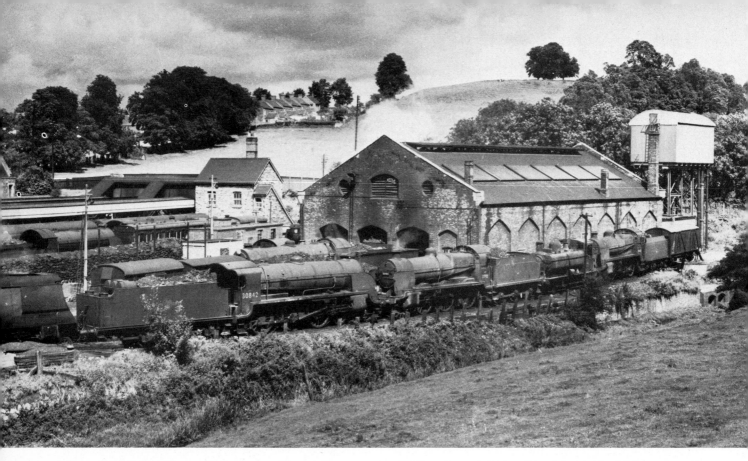

Yeovil Motive Power Depôt

86 *Above:* A panoramic view of Yeovil shed. A rising field just to the south made a wonderful 'grandstand' from which to watch shed activities.

87 *Below:* M7 0-4-4T No 30129 and S15 4-6-0 No 30846.

88 *Above:* S15 No 30843. This was one of the final batch of ten engines of this class built in 1936.

89 *Below:* 'Battle of Britain' Pacific No 34051 *Winston Churchill*, just ex-works and positively gleaming in the winter sunshine, stands outside Yeovil shed on 3 November 1963.

A Brief Detour Down the Yeovil-Dorchester Line

This line was planned as a part of the Wilts, Somerset & Weymouth Railway, but long before it was completed in 1857, the WS & WR had been taken over by the Great Western Railway. When the railways of Britain were nationalised in 1948 the line became part of the Southern Region. In 1962 however, there was a major re-shuffle of the regional boundaries, and this line, together with the old Southern main line from Salisbury westwards, found itself in the grasp of the Western Region.

90 *Above:* T9 No 30718, heading south from Yeovil with an enthusiasts' special, has just passed underneath the Southern main line east of Yeovil Junction and is approaching the start of the $5\frac{1}{2}$ mile climb, on a ruling gradient of 1 in 51, up to the summit at Evershot.

91 *Left:* The 11.10am (SO) Wolverhampton to Weymouth, in the charge of an ex-Great Western 'Hall' class 4-6-0, climbing up through the deep cutting leading to Evershot Tunnel, and the end of the arduous climb from Yeovil. Giving rear-end assistance — but not yet in view in this picture — was a Southern U class 2-6-0.

Evershot

The summit of the climb from Yeovil is at the southern end of Evershot Tunnel, a short distance beyond which was Evershot station.

92 *Above:* On an overcast and dismal Saturday in August 1964, ex-GWR 4-6-0 No 6830 *Buckenhill Grange* emerges from Evershot Tunnel with the 11.10am (SO) Wolverhampton-Weymouth . . .

93 *Left:* . . . to be followed by U class 2-6-0 No 31792, pushing heartily in the rear.

94 *Left:* As the train passed over the summit, the U dropped away from the rear, and came to a stand just beyond the station. The engine then reversed over a trailing crossover on to the up road, but was held for a while by signals before she could return downhill to Yeovil.

Maiden Newton — and another 'Eastern Invasion'

95 *Above:* Ex-LNER Gresley A4 Pacific No 60024 *Kingfisher* passing through Maiden Newton on 26 March 1966, as she climbed towards Evershot with a special organised by the A4 Preservation Society.

96 *Left:* Even judged by normal English summer weather, 25 August 1963, was an appalling day. Drenching rain poured down incessantly from a leaden sky, and by mid afternoon a heavy mist had begun to envelop the countryside. All very hard luck on the Southern Counties Touring Association, for this was the day they were running one of their most enterprising excursions, and an ex-LNER Pacific, A3 No 60112 *St Simon*, had been brought over specially from the Eastern Region to haul the train.

In the late afternoon, and with the rain still pouring down, *St Simon* and her train set off from Maiden Newton into the growing gloom for the run up to Yeovil. (See Plate 181).

The Bridport Branch

From Maiden Newton a branch line set off south west to run down to Bridport and, originally, West Bay. For several years prior to closure in 1975, the branch was worked by a DMU, but up to 1966, steam frequently visited the line on enthusiasts' specials.

97 *Above:* Two Ivatt 2-6-2 tanks, Nos 41301 and 41284 in charge of a Locomotive Club of Great Britain special, set their train back on to the down road prior to a run down the branch to Bridport on 27 February 1966.

98 *Left:* To avoid problems with running round at Bridport, the LCGB special on 27 February 1966, was worked down the branch with an Ivatt tank at either end. In this picture they are drawing near to Maiden Newton on the return run from Bridport.

Back on the Southern main line — Crewkerne

On 24 April 1953, Crewkerne was the scene of a highly dramatic incident when 'Merchant Navy' Pacific No 35020, travelling at high speed, fractured her driving axle. As a result, all thirty engines of the class were withdrawn from service for examination, and during the emergency, several locomotives were borrowed from other Regions. (See also Plate 71).

99 *Above:* Amongst the locomotives lent by the Eastern Region was V2 2-6-2 No 60928, seen here passing Crewkerne with the third portion of the down 'Atlantic Coast Express' on 23 May 1953. Whilst on loan to the Southern Region, No 60928 was shedded at Nine Elms MPD.

100 *Below:* The Western Region came to the rescue with 'Britannia' Pacifics. On 23 May 1953, the second portion of the down 'Atlantic Coast Express' passed through Crewkerne hauled by No 70029 *Shooting Star*, on loan to Exmouth Junction MPD from Cardiff (Canton) shed.

High Speed
East of Axminster

From Salisbury to Exeter, the Southern West-of-England main line is a series of sweeping undulations, downhill stretches being followed by banks of increasing length and severity as the line progresses westwards. The climax comes just after Crewkerne; for 13 miles the line now sweeps downhill, but then follows the most severe test of all — Honiton Bank. This starts a little over a mile west of Axminster. First comes $1\frac{3}{4}$ miles of 1 in 100, then $4\frac{1}{2}$ miles of 1 in 80, and finally $\frac{3}{4}$ mile of 1 in 132 through Honiton Tunnel.

   With Axminster close to the bottom of the dip, in the days of steam westbound expresses would come down through the station, travelling like the wind, to get up all the impetus they could for the coming attack on the dreaded ascent up to Honiton Tunnel. Equally well, eastbound expresses, after a whirlwind descent of Honiton Bank, were still travelling very fast as they tore through Axminster and climbed towards Crewkerne.

101 *Above:* On 5 September 1959, 'West Country' Pacific No 34034 *Honiton* seemed to know that her own bank — Honiton — lay ahead, for she must have been travelling at well over 80mph as she came streaking down towards Axminster with a West-of-England express.

102 *Below:* Heading east out of the storm, 'Merchant Navy' Pacific No 35003 *Royal Mail* — still in original condition — comes thundering up the bank from Axminster with an eastbound express.

Axminster

At Axminster a branch line diverged to run south for seven miles through enchanting country to the seaside resort of Lyme Regis. Branch line trains set off heading southwest from a bay platform on the *up* side. Immediately after the start they made a steep climbing turn to the south to pass over the main line before commencing to wend their way towards Lyme Regis.

103 *Above:* On a murky morning in March 1959, Adams 4-4-2T No 30582 sits quietly in the bay platform with the branch train, whilst 'West Country' Pacific No 34006 *Bude*, unhappy in the light drizzle, slips violently as she endeavours to get her westbound express under way again.

104 *Below:* A pair of Ivatt 2-6-2 tanks, Nos 41291 and 41206, standing in Axminster up platform with an excursion train which they later took down the branch to Lyme Regis.

105 *Above:* Adams 4-4-2T No 30583 setting off with the branch train for Lyme Regis. Happily, this Adams tank is still 'alive'. Resplendent in L&SWR livery, and carrying her old number 488, she is now running on the Bluebell Railway in Sussex.

106 *Below:* Two small ex-Great Western 0-4-2 tanks, Nos 1442 and 1450, pause a while at Axminster to take water whilst on their way from Yeovil to Exmouth Junction shed on Sunday, 7 February 1965. (See also Plates 76 and 125).

The Axminster–Lyme Regis Branch

For many years the Adams 4-4-2 tanks held undisputed sway on the branch. At various times several other types of engine had been tried out as replacements for the ageing Adams, but without success. Either they damaged the track due to their wheelbase not being sufficiently flexible for the many sharp curves on the branch, or they had not got the power to cope with the 1 in 40 gradients. Eventually, in 1961, a suitable replacement was found at last — an ex-LMS Ivatt 2-6-2 tank was tried out, and proved a success. So the long reign of the Adams tanks on the Axminster-Lyme Regis branch came to an end.

107 *Above:* Adams 4-4-2T No-30582 has just crossed Cannington viaduct and is heading north with a return working from Lyme Regis to Axminster in early spring 1959.

108 *Below:* On a glorious summer's evening in June 1960, a pair of Adams tanks, Nos 30584 and 30583, climb towards Combpyne with the 5.40pm from Axminster.

109 *Below:* On summer Saturdays there used to be a through working of coaches between Waterloo and Lyme Regis. As this regularly loaded to five bogies of heavy main line stock, the train was always double-headed by two of the Adams tanks. In this picture Nos 30582 — still with a Drummond boiler and valves on the dome — and 30583 are plodding uphill past Shapwick Grange farm with the return working from Lyme Regis to Waterloo on 12 September 1959.

110 *Bottom:* The engine that finally ousted the elderly Adams tanks from the branch was Ivatt's 2-6-2 tank, designed for the LMS in 1946. In February 1965 the service between Axminster and Lyme Regis was being worked by one of these engines, No 41216, and an ex-Great Western rail motor coach; they are seen here dropping downhill towards Cannington viaduct.

Seaton Junction

After 1½ miles of climbing Honiton Bank, one used to come to Seaton Junction — but sadly now no longer a junction since the lifting of the branch line that ran from the station down to the seaside resort of Seaton. Through the station the line was quadruple track, the up and down mains having a clear run through the middle, with loops forming the platform roads.

111 *Above:* 'Battle of Britain' Pacific No 34059, *Sir Archibald Sinclair*, pulls out from the up platform with the 11.48am Plymouth to Waterloo, whilst a westbound local stands in the down platform.

112 *Below:* The Seaton branch trains used the outer face of the down platform. In recent times the branch service had been run with DMUs, but early in 1965 a sudden dearth of DMUs in the West Country led to two small ex-Great Western 0-4-2 tanks being hastily borrowed from Yeovil shed to work the service for a short while. No 1442 is seen here about to set off from the Junction with her one-coach train for Seaton.

The Seaton Branch

This branch line was in sharp contrast to the Axminster-Lyme Regis branch. The run of just over four miles was easily graded and there were no curves of any consequence.

113 *Above:* Ex-Great Western 0-4-2T No 1442 with her one coach, makes a smart departure from Colyton for the run down to Seaton on 27 February 1965 . . .

114 *Left:* . . . and rests awhile in Seaton station at the end of the run.

Honiton Bank

115 *Above:* The 22 August 1964, was a most perfect summer's day and as a railway enthusiast, I could not have wished for a more delightful spot to spend it than near the top of Honiton Bank where the line climbs up through a deep wooded cutting towards the entrance to the tunnel. With the nearest main road over half a mile away, nothing disturbed the peace and tranquility of this beautiful spot, and all day I sat in the shade of the trees and watched the procession of summer Saturday trains pass by.

Early in the afternoon, 'West Country' Pacific No 34023 *Blackmore Vale* came on the scene, making an excellent climb with the 10.15am (SO) Waterloo to Ilfracombe. Happily this is another Bulleid Pacific which is still 'alive'. Beautifully restored, and immaculate in her original Southern Railway livery, *Blackmore Vale* is now running on the Bluebell Railway, and so is a stable companion of Adams 4-4-2 tank No 488.

116 *Right:* Externally, No 34110
66 Squadron was in a pretty grubbty
state, but she sounded in excellent
mechanical condition as she came
quickly up the bank with the three-
coach 1.18pm (Sunday) Salisbury to
Exeter on 3 September 1961.

117 *Below:* In the haze of an early
autumn day, 'Battle of Britain' Pacific
No 34057 *Biggin Hill* makes a steady
climb with the 11.30am (Sunday)
Brighton to Plymouth. This through
working of 200 miles was the longest
continuous locomotive working on
the Southern Region.

Honiton
Tunnel —
The Eastern
End

118 *Above:* 'Battle of Britain' Pacific
No 34056 *Croydon*, about to enter
the tunnel with the 9am (SO)
Waterloo to Exmouth on 22 August
1964.

119 *Right:* Another of the many
pictures I took on 22 August 1964.
BR Standard Class 5 4-6-0 No 73030
drifts out of the tunnel and down the
bank with the 11am Plymouth to
Brighton.

120 *Above:* 'Merchant Navy' Pacific
No 35001 *Channel Packet*, — just
ex-works and resplendent in a new
coat of fresh green paint — climbing
vigorously up the final length of
1 in 80 towards the tunnel with the
heavy Surbiton-Okehampton car ferry
train on 22 August 1964.

121 *Right:* A down goods train,
hauled by 'Battle of Britain' Pacific
No 34081 *92 Squadron,* comes
slowly up through the autumn mist
towards the tunnel on a bleak day in
early October 1963.

Honiton Tunnel —
The Western End

122 *Above:* No 34108 *Wincanton* emerges slowly into the summer sunshine again with the 11.45am (SO) Waterloo to Ilfracombe. The final $\frac{3}{4}$ mile of 1 in 132 through the tunnel had brought *Wincanton* down to around 30mph but her struggle was over, for the summit of the seven mile climb comes right at the western end of the tunnel.

123 *Below:* A busy day for *Channel Packet.* On the morning of 22 August 1964, she had worked down to Exeter the heavy Surbiton-Okehampton car ferry train. (See Plate 120). And in the afternoon, here she is climbing the final stretch of 1 in 90 up to Honiton Tunnel with the 11.48am Plymouth to Waterloo, which she had taken over at Exeter.

From Honiton Tunnel the line starts to sweep downhill at 1 in 90. After easing to 1 in 300 through Honiton, the descent continues westwards at 1 in 100 for another three miles before a brief rise to Sidmouth Junction. Then, with one slight 'hiccup', the next eight miles are all on a falling grade.

124 *Top:* 'Lord Nelson' class 4-6-0s were never widely used on the Salisbury-Exeter main line. This is No 30861 *Lord Anson* climbing towards Honiton Tunnel with the return working of an enthusiasts' special on 2 September 1962.

125 *Above:* Our two small friends, ex-Great Western 0-4-2 tanks Nos 1442 and 1450, emerge from Honiton Tunnel into the fast-failing light of a dull winter's afternoon, during the course of their journey down the main line from Yeovil to Exmouth Junction shed on Sunday, 7 February 1965. (See Plates 76 and 106).

Sidmouth Junction

The Sidmouth branch set off south east from a bay platform on the down side to run for eight miles, through Ottery St Mary and Tipton St John's, down to Sidmouth on the coast. At Tipton St John's, a line diverged to head south for six and a half miles to Budleigh Salterton, and then continued on west for a further four miles to Exmouth.

126 *Above:* In 1955 the Southern Region was allocated 20 BR Standard Class 5 4-6-0s, Nos 73080-89 and 73110-19. Initially, like the Standard Class 5s on all the other Regions, these engines were unnamed. But with the withdrawal of the 'King Arthur' class, names — but not the nameplates — previously carried by 'King Arthurs', were transferred to the SR's 20 Standard Class 5s. Heading east from Sidmouth Junction with an up parcels train on 2 September 1962, is No 73115, which was named *King Pellinore* in February 1960.

The Sidmouth branch can be seen swinging away to the left of this picture.

127 *Below:* After a brief pause at Sidmouth Junction, 'Schools' class 4-4-0 No 30925 *Cheltenham*, gets away again with an up stopping train. Passing through the station on the down line is an S15, running light engine tender-first, whilst an Ivatt 2-6-2T sits in the bay platform with a train for Sidmouth.

128 *Above:* 'Lord Nelson' class 4-6-0 No 30861 *Lord Anson*, arriving with an enthusiasts' special which she had brought down from Waterloo on 2 September 1962. The train was to run down the branch, hauled by the two M7 tanks seen waiting on the right of this picture.

129 *Below:* For many years, much of the traffic on the branch had been handled by Drummond's M7 0-4-4 tanks, until they were superseded by Ivatt and BR 2-6-2 tanks. On 2 September 1962, two M7s, Nos 30025 and 30024, hauled an enthusiasts' special over the branch. (See Plate above.) Here they are, making a very spirited climb of the steep bank which lay between Budleigh Salterton and Exmouth.

Exmouth Junction
Motive Power Depôt

130 *Above:* A general panoramic view of the Running Shed.

131 *Left:* A contrast in tank engines. No 30956, a Maunsell Z class 0-8-0T of 1929, faces No 30584, one of Adams' 4-4-2 tanks, a class first introduced in 1882.

132 *Below left:* Z Class 0-8-0T. No 30953 and Drummond '700' class 0-6-0 No 30317.

133 *Right:* Two Maunsell N class 2-6-0s, Nos 31841 and 31836.

134 *Below right:* 'Battle of Britain' Pacific No 34072 *257 Squadron* standing alongside the shed on 24 April 1960.

Exeter Central

The line from Salisbury to Yeovil was completed on 1 June 1860, and seven weeks later the extension on to Exeter was opened on 19 July 1860. A happy programme was laid on at Exeter Central station on 19 July 1960, to celebrate the Centenary. Three engines were on display in the station yard, all immaculately turned out, and with their footplates open for inspection by the public. In the afternoon one of the little Beattie 2-4-0 well tanks, hauling a short train, ran in from St James Park Halt to make a ceremonial arrival at Exeter Central. The locomotive crew and all the passengers were in period costume for the occasion.

At one stage during the day, the heavens opened and rain poured down in torrents but this did not dampen the ardour of the many spectators who had come along to enjoy the event.

135/136 *Above:* The three engines on display — Bulleid 'Merchant Navy' Pacific No 35003 *Royal Mail* (built 1941, modified 1959), Adams 4-4-2T No 30582 (1883), and Beattie 2-4-0WT No 30587 (1874).

137 *Above:* Beattie 2-4-0WT No 30587 and her train make a ceremonial arrival at Exeter Central on the afternoon of 19 July 1960. The Beattie's train, with which she had made the short journey from St James Park Halt, consisted of the ex-L&SWR two-car 'Gate' set off the Yeovil Town branch, plus a third coach.

138 *Below:* The little Beattie stands proudly in Exeter Central after arrival, whilst her driver — attired in period costume and obviously enjoying the whole affair — looks out happily from the cab.

Part Two Bournemouth to Weymouth

Bournemouth Motive Power Depôt

139 *Above:* From the western end of the down platform of Bournemouth Central station — the second longest platform in the country — one had a marvellous view of Bournemouth shed. In this picture, the engines 'on view' are rebuilt 'Battle of Britain' and 'West Country' Pacifics, and BR Standard Class 4s and Class 5s.

Bournemouth Central

140 *Above:* The eastern end of the station. 'Battle of Britain' Pacific No 34076 *41 Squadron*, still in original condition, stands in the middle road, whilst rebuilt 'Merchant Navy' Pacific No 35022 *Holland America Line*, which had brought in an up local train from Weymouth, draws forward under the authorisation of the Shunt-Ahead signal, prior to setting back and berthing the coaches in the station on the down through road.

141 *Left:* The western end of the station. 'West Country' Pacific No 34001 *Exeter* sets off with the 10.30am Waterloo to Weymouth. In this picture, just visible above the left-hand arm of the bracket signal, is the station's roof top signalbox.

Bournemouth Central

DEPARTURE

142 *Above:* Amidst swirling smoke and steam, No 35012 *United States Line* makes an impressive departure with an up express on 25 April 1964.

AND ARRIVALS

143 *Above:* In warm autumn sunshine on a day in early October 1965, No 34076 *41 Squadron* emerges from under the road bridge at the east end of the station, to run in with a down express from Waterloo.

144 *Below:* During a heavy shower on 25 April 1964, 'Merchant Navy' Pacific No 35017 *Belgian Marine* appeared through the rain, drifting in with the 11.30am, Weymouth to Waterloo. Standing on the right is M7 0-4-4T. No 30480, waiting to attach the Bournemouth West portion on to the rear of 35017 and her train.

Between Bournemouth Central and Bournemouth West

145 *Above:* On a misty morning in early April 1964, M7 0-4-4T No 30480 draws forward some empty stock from the sidings just to the west of Bournemouth Central station.

146 *Below:* 'West Country' Pacific No 34048 *Crediton*, running tender-first, passes by, light engine, on her way from Bournemouth West to Bournemouth Shed.

The departure westwards from Bournemouth Central station is a most attractive piece of railway, the line running for some distance in a shallow cutting bordered on both sides by clusters of pine trees.

147 *Above:* On a fine morning in early June 1964, 'Merchant Navy' Pacific No 35028 *Clan Line*, draws near to Bournemouth Central with the 9.25am Weymouth to Waterloo. This is the 'Merchant Navy' which, happily, is still 'alive'. Most beautifully restored by the Merchant Navy Preservation Society, *Clan Line* is at present living with the famous ex-Great Western engine *King George V* at Bulmer's railway centre, at Hereford.

Between Bournemouth Central and Bournemouth West

148 *Above:* The 12.20pm Bournemouth West to Waterloo being hauled for the first 3½ miles of the journey as far as Bournemouth Central, by BR 2-6-2T No 82028. At Bournemouth Central, the train will be attached to the rear of the 11.30am Weymouth-Waterloo. (See Plate 144).

149 *Left:* 'Lord Nelson' class 4-6-0 No 30857 *Lord Howe*, heading west from Bournemouth Central with the 11.30am Waterloo-Bournemouth West semi-fast on 3 October 1959. For many years, up to 1960, this was a regular 'Lord Nelson' duty.

150 *Above:* Our friend *Clan Line* again. This time No 35028 is running between Bournemouth Central and Bournemouth West with the down 'Bournemouth Belle'.

Bournemouth West

Although the terminus of Bournemouth West was less than 1½ miles away from Bournemouth Central 'as the seagull flies', the distance by rail between the two stations was 3½ miles. Down trains for Bournemouth West set off from Bournemouth Central travelling west past Meyrick Park, and then at Gas Works Junction, did a 'U' turn to take them back east again and down a steep bank into Bournemouth West. The descent into the terminus at 1 in 101, and finally 1 in 90, called for considerable care, and in bad weather, a greasy rail often made departure from Bournemouth West with a heavy train, something of an ordeal for enginemen.

Bournemouth West was closed in October 1965, and today nothing remains of this once busy and attractive six-platform terminus.

151 *Above:* Two 'King Arthurs' at Bournemouth West in August 1954. On the left, No 30746 *Pendragon*, takes water, whilst sister engine No 30738 *King Pellinore*, in charge of an up express for Waterloo, blows off vigorously whilst waiting for the road.

152 *Below:* 'Lord Nelson' class 4-6-0 No 30865 *Sir John Hawkins* climbing steadily up the bank out of Bournemouth West with the 11.10am express for Waterloo on 4 August 1954. Standing on the left is H15 class 4-6-0 No 30490.

153 *Above:* Bournemouth West was also the terminus for Somerset & Dorset trains. The Somerset and Dorset's own line ended at Broadstone and from there, S&D trains ran over the Southern line for the last eight miles of their journey into Bournemouth.

On 14 August 1954, S&D 7F 2-8-0 No 53807 makes a rousing start out of the terminus with the 12 o'clock relief to Tunstall, whilst in the adjacent platform, 'King Arthur' No 30744 *Maid of Astolat*, at the head of the 12.10pm to Waterloo, waits impatiently for her turn to leave.

154 *Right:* Seven years later, on 2 July 1961, 'King Arthur' No 30765 *Sir Gareth*, stands quietly in the station, waiting to leave with the 1.06pm (Sundays) stopping train to Southampton Central.

Bournemouth West

155 *Top:* The 30 March 1964, was a dreary day. As No 34045 *Ottery St Mary* waited to leave with the 2.10pm relief to Waterloo, a bitter east wind swept through the station — and summer still seemed a long way away . . .

156 *Above:* . . . and even after summer had officially arrived, the weather often wasn't much better. On an overcast day in early June 1964, No 34001 *Exeter* drifts down the bank into Bournemouth West with the 12.14pm from Waterloo.

The 'Bournemouth Belle'

This luxurious, all-Pullman train, running between London and Bournemouth, was first introduced in the summer of 1931. Initially the 'Bournemouth Belle' ran only during the summer months, but by 1936 the service had become so popular that the train ran daily throughout the year. After being withdrawn for the duration of World War II, the 'Bournemouth Belle' commenced running again in 1946, and continued in service until 1967 when it was phased out with the completion of the electrification of the London-Bournemouth main line. At the height of the summer season, the 'Belle' would load up to 12 Pullmans — 490 tons tare and well over 500 tons full — and was the heaviest train regularly to be worked out of Bournemouth West. Right up until 1966 the train was hauled by steam — usually a 'Merchant Navy' Pacific — and it was only in the last few months of service that the 'Bournemouth Belle' succumbed to diesel traction.

157 *Above:* 'Let battle commence!' — 'West Country' Pacific No 34021 *Dartmoor*, gets away cleanly with the up 'Bournemouth Belle' on a summer's day in 1965.

The luggage van of the 'Bournemouth Belle' — seen here next to the engine — was an ex-Great Western vehicle, which had been specially painted in the brown and cream Pullman livery so as to match the rest of the train.

158 *Right:* The engine which brought in the empty stock of the up 'Bournemouth Belle', used to give rear end assistance up the steep bank out of Bournemouth West. On this occasion, Ivatt 2-6-2T, No 41293 certainly played her full part in ensuring the smooth departure of the 'Belle'.

Parkstone Bank

Parkstone Bank starts a mile to the east of Poole station. For 1½ miles the line climbs steeply eastwards at 1 in 60, with only a brief easing to 1 in 300 through Parkstone station. Then follows a short 'breather' at 1 in 990, and finally ¾ mile at 1 in 130.

159 *Above:* On a hot afternoon in late June 1964, BR Standard Class 5 No 73018, with nine on, was making an excellent climb of the bank as she passed by in charge of the 12.10pm from Weymouth.

160 *Below:* 'Battle of Britain' Pacific No 34071 *601 Squadron*, drifts down the bank with the 8.35am Waterloo to Weymouth on 3 August 1964.

In the days of steam, the deep cutting a little to the east of Parkstone station made a delightful spot from which to watch the trains. When I look at my pictures taken at this location, memories come flooding back; of hot summer days, sitting in the shade of the trees, amidst clumps of purple heather, the air heavy with the fragrant scent of the pines. All would be peaceful and quiet. Then suddenly, above the soft sighing of the wind through the pines, would come the faint but unmistakeable sound of a hard-working steam locomotive — a train was coming up the bank! The heavy, striving beat grew steadily louder. A momentary muffling of the exhaust would indicate that the engine had just passed underneath the bridge at the east end of Parkstone station, and then she would come slowly into sight round the bend, toiling up the 1 in 60 bank with her train.

161 *Above:* 'Child's play!' 'Merchant Navy' No 35001 *Channel Packet*, in charge of the 11.30am Weymouth to Waterloo, romps up the bank at speed with her light load of four coaches and a van. However, at Bournemouth Central the train would be considerably increased in weight by the addition of the portion from Bournemouth West . . .

162 *Below:* . . . But a little later, M7 0-4-4T No 30111, with the 12.08pm 'Push and Pull' from Brockenhurst, wasn't sounding nearly as happy as she passed slowly by, propelling her two coaches up the bank.

Parkstone Bank — A Contrast in Tank Engines

163 *Above:* BR Standard Class 4 2-6-4T No 80147, a type first introduced in 1951, climbs the bank with the 12.10pm Weymouth to Bournemouth on 5 August 1963.

164 *Below:* Later in the afternoon, the 2.35pm Bournemouth West to Brockenhurst 'Push and Pull' via Ringwood and West Moors came drifting down the bank behind 0-4-4T No 30048, one of the M7 class designed by Drummond for the L&SWR in 1897.

Parkstone Bay

165 *Right:* 'King Arthur' class 4-6-0 No 30740 *Merlin*, making a vigorous start on the 1 in 60 of Parkstone Bank, skirts the waters of Parkstone Bay with an up stopping train from Weymouth on 2 August 1954. Today this scene is totally different, for the land to the south of the line has been reclaimed, and the waters of Parkstone Bay no longer lap the foot of the railway embankment. However, to make up for the loss of this attraction, the gas works in the background has been demolished!

Holes Bay Junction

166 *Below:* After sweeping round the causeway from Hamworthy Junction, the 10.10am from Weymouth, hauled by BR Class 4 2-6-0 No 76005, passes Holes Bay Junction on a misty, cold day in March 1964. The line coming in from the right is from Broadstone.

Poole

After the descent of Parkstone Bank, the line begins turning north west in a long, sweeping curve towards Poole. Just before reaching the station the railway used to pass over two level-crossings — the cause of monumental traffic jams during the summer months — but the major one of these was replaced by an over bridge in 1971. The curvature at the approach and through the station is severe, with continuous lengths of check rail. An interesting working feature was that right up until 1961, it was compulsory for all trains to stop at Poole.

167 *Above:* 'Merchant Navy' Pacific No 35024 *East Asiatic Company*, running west, light engine, negotiates the severe curve through Poole station. Note the continuous check rail.

168 *Left:* There used to be two level-crossings in Poole in quick succession, the first, and very busy one, immediately to the east of the station, and the second some 100 yards further on. On a dismal winter's day in 1964, BR 2-6-2T No 82029 approaches the second, and now sole remaining, crossing with an eastbound stopping train.

Poole Quay

169/170: From Poole goods yard, a line used to run through the streets for nearly half a mile to Poole Quay. All movements along the public road and on the quay were made with extreme caution, a flagman walking ahead of the engine (*above*) to warn road traffic.

With the shadows lengthening on a warm summer's evening in early August 1954, B4 0-4-0T No 30093 completes her shunting on the quay and (*below*) sets off carefully for the return run through the streets to the main line. (The flagman, walking ahead of the train, is just out of the picture on the left hand side.)

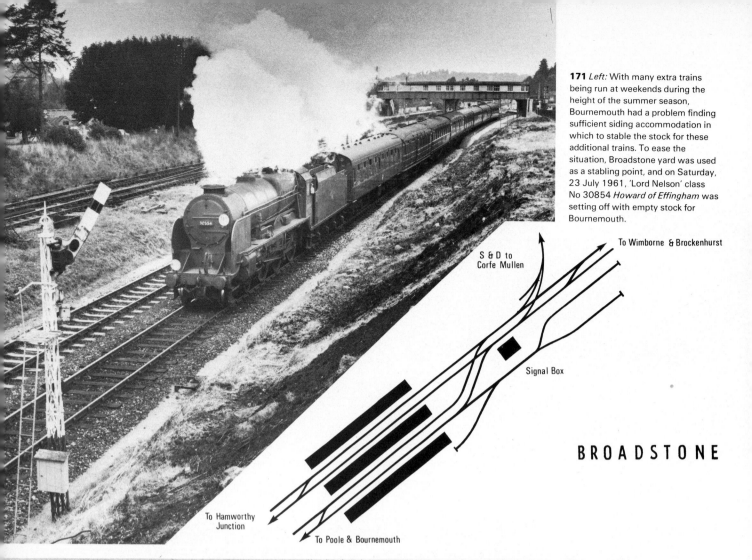

171 *Left:* With many extra trains being run at weekends during the height of the summer season, Bournemouth had a problem finding sufficient siding accommodation in which to stable the stock for these additional trains. To ease the situation, Broadstone yard was used as a stabling point, and on Saturday, 23 July 1961, 'Lord Nelson' class No 30854 *Howard of Effingham* was setting off with empty stock for Bournemouth.

S & D to Corfe Mullen

To Wimborne & Brockenhurst

Signal Box

To Hamworthy Junction

To Poole & Bournemouth

BROADSTONE

Broadstone

172 *Left:* M7 0-4-4T No 30108 leaves Broadstone with a stopping train for Brockenhurst. The line passing straight through the station, ran to Hamworthy Junction, whilst the Poole line can be seen bearing off to the left just behind the signalbox. Leading out of the picture on the right hand side is the Somerset & Dorset's single-line to Corfe Mullen.

175 *Right:* Q class 0-6-0 No 30548 comes in off the Wimborne line on 18 April 1964, with an enthusiast's special organised by the Locomotive Club of Great Britain.

173 *Above:* During the height of the summer service, some Waterloo-Weymouth trains by-passed Bournemouth. Bearing west at Lymington Junction, they ran through Ringwood and Wimborne to Broadstone, from where they dropped down to Hamworthy Junction to rejoin the main line. On 16 July 1960, 'West Country' Pacific No 34039 *Boscastle*, takes the Hamworthy line at Broadstone with a down Waterloo-Weymouth express.

174 *Below:* On a wet summer Saturday in 1961, 'Schools' class 4-4-0 No 30905 *Tonbridge*, pulls out of Broadstone yard with a train of empty stock composed of ex-LNER coaches. Note the articulated pair next to the engine.

Broadstone

176 *Above:* In the late afternoon of 7 August 1954, T9 4-4-0 No 30721 departs from Broadstone with a stopping train to Salisbury.

177 *Below:* S&D 7F 2-8-0 No 53808 comes off the Somerset & Dorset's single-line section from Corfe Mullen with the 7.43am (SO) Birmingham to Bournemouth on 7 August 1954. The arm of the mechanical tablet catcher (seen on the right, level with 53808's buffer beam) has been swung out to collect from the engine the single-line token for the Corfe Mullen-Broadstone section.

178 *Above:* On a fine summer's morning in mid-July 1960, M7 0-4-4T No 30108 sets off towards Wimborne with a stopping train to Brockenhurst. . . .

179 *Below:* . . . and three years later, on a sultry afternoon in early August 1963, another M7 with a local bound for Brockenhurst, rumbles across the bridge over the river Stour just west of Wimborne.

Hamworthy Junction — on a *very* wet day!

180 *Above:* The weather on Sunday, 25 August 1963, was appalling. For hour after hour drenching rain poured down from a leaden sky and, driven by a strong wind, soon made nonsense of any so-called raincoat. I don't think I ever got so wet trying to take pictures of trains!

With water streaming from the carriage roofs, a down express comes round the curve from Holes Bay, hauled by 'West Country' Pacific No 34024 *Tamar Valley*. Coming in on the left hand side of the picture is the line from Broadstone.

181 *Below:* On 25 August 1963, the Southern Counties Touring Society were running one of their special excursion trains, and a big attraction of this one was the motive power — an ex-LNER Gresley A3 Pacific. The locomotive, No 60112 *St Simon*, had been brought over from the Eastern Region specially to haul the train, and was used for all the main-line sections of the run. The excursion traversed several branch lines, including the goods-only line down to Hamworthy over which the Pacific was not permitted to run. So whilst an M7 tank worked the train down to Hamworthy and back, *St Simon* waited dejectedly in the pouring rain at Hamworthy Junction. (See also Plates 96 and 208).

182 *Right:* No 1, *Bonnie Prince Charlie*, built by Robert Stephenson & Hawthorns Ltd, in 1949, works number 7544.

Hamworthy Quay

Poole's first station, built in 1847, was at Hamworthy Quay. Then in 1872 a new and more conveniently situated station was opened in Poole. Passenger traffic on the Hamworthy line soon began to fade, and since 1896 the line has been used solely for goods traffic. One of the companies at Hamworthy, Southern Wharves Ltd, used to shunt their sidings with their own steam locomotives, and in 1949 acquired two new engines built by Robert Stephenson & Hawthorns Ltd.

These attractive little 0–4–0 saddle tanks, numbered 1 and 2, bore the names *Bonnie Prince Charlie* and *Western Pride*. After being taken out of service, No 2 was scrapped, but happily No 1 *Bonnie Prince Charlie* is now preserved at the Great Western Society's depôt at Didcot.

184 *Right:* No 2 *Western Pride*, built by Robert Stephenson & Hawthorns Ltd, in 1949, works number 7545.

Wareham

An easy five-mile run through the flat heathland of south Dorset, brings the line to Wareham station, situated some half-mile to the north of this ancient Anglo-Saxon town of great charm.

185 *Above:* After a brief pause at Wareham on 7 May 1961, 'Merchant Navy' Pacific No 35019 *French Line CGT*, sets off for Weymouth with the 1.30pm (Sundays) from Waterloo.

186 *Below:* M7 0-4-4T No 30060, propelling her two-coach train, puffs busily away from Wareham towards Worgret Junction and the Swanage branch.

The Swanage Branch

The Swanage branch diverges from the main line at Worgret Junction 1¼ miles west of Wareham. The line then turns south east to run for ten miles through the Isle of Purbeck, past Furzebrook and Corfe Castle, down to Swanage on the coast. For many years, in the days of steam, the branch service was worked by M7 0-4-4 tanks, trains being propelled down to Swanage, and then coming back to Wareham, engine-first.

187 *Right:* The 3.58pm from Swanage, hauled by M7 0-4-4T No 30328, passing Worgret Junction Distant signal on a dull Sunday in late August 1961.

188 *Below:* M7 No 30060 running north west from Furzebrook on a glorious afternoon in early May 1961, with a return working from Swanage to Wareham.

The Swanage Branch

Passenger service over the branch came to an end in January 1972. However, the 2½ miles from Worgret Junction down as far as Furzebrook remain in use carrying traffic from the ECC Clay Works and in the spring of 1977 came the interesting news that Furzebrook had been chosen as the Southern Region railhead to handle 200,000 tons of oil annually from the important oilfield recently discovered in the Isle of Purbeck.

There is also great activity on the railway enthusiasts front; the Swanage Railway Society is making strenuous efforts to be allowed to restore a passenger carrying service between Swanage and Wareham.

189 *Above:* Towards the end of steam, many enthusiasts' specials were run down the Swanage branch. This one was organised by the Locomotive Club of Great Britain and is seen heading north west past Corfe Castle on 27 February 1966, hauled by a pair of Ivatt 2-6-2 tanks, Nos 41301 and 41284. (Later in the day, the same train traversed the Bridport banch — see Plates 97 and 98).

190 *Right:* The Isle of Purbeck has long been famous for its deposits of ball clay. Two firms working the clay were B. Fayle & Co at Norden, and Pike Brothers & Co at Furzebrook. In 1949 they amalgamated to form Pike Bros, Fayle & Co Ltd, a company which, in turn, has now been incorporated in ECC Ball Clays Ltd. At both Norden and Furzebrook, narrow gauge tramways were used to carry the clay from the workings to the weathering beds, and from there to sidings on the Swanage branch line.

This is 'Russell' on the 2ft gauge line at Norden. She was built originally for the North Wales Narrow Gauge Railway Co by Hunslet & Co in 1906. Happily 'Russell' has been preserved, and is now back home again in North Wales.

The Furzebrook Railway

The 2ft 8in gauge system of Pike Bros, popularly known as the Furzebrook Railway*, was considerably more extensive than that at Norden. Several attractive small steam locomotives worked this charming little railway which ran across the Dorset heathland. On the way out to the mine at West Creech, some three miles from Furzebrook, the line passed through a small wood near Grange Gate — an enchanting spot on a fine summer's day.

Sadly the Furzebrook Railway is no longer in existence. Road transport began to replace the railway in 1955, and the line finally came to an end in 1957.

*Profusely illustrated in my book *The Narrow Gauge Charm of Yesterday*, published by the Oxford Publishing Company.

191 *Right:* A fine summer's morning in August 1954. 'Quintus', an 0-4-0 saddle tank built by Manning Wardle & Co in 1914, is on her way, light-engine, to West Creech to collect a train of clay . . .

192 *Below:* . . . and here she is, later in the morning, coming back in leisurely fashion through the countryside with her train-load of clay, and about to enter the woods near Grange Gate.

East of Moreton

After the virtually level run from Poole to Wareham, the next 15 miles to Dorchester are chiefly on a rising grade. As the line runs westwards, the uphill stretches become more severe, the last 4½ miles to Moreton steepening from 1 in 400 to 1 in 200, and then to 1 in 100 over the final mile.

193 *Above:* 10 June 1967. The end of steam on the Southern Region was only one month away as 'Merchant Navy' Pacific No 35028 *Clan Line* — with her nameplates already removed prior to withdrawal — came swiftly down the bank east of Moreton with the 4pm up Channel Islands boat train from Weymouth to Waterloo.

194 *Below:* The preserved ex-LNER Gresley A4 Pacific No 4498 *Sir Nigel Gresley*, climbing towards Moreton on 4 June 1967, with an enthusiasts' special from Waterloo to Weymouth.

Dorchester

Prior to nationalisation, the Southern Railway's own line ended at
Dorchester, for there was a junction here with the Great Western
Railway, and it was over GWR track that Southern trains travelled to
reach Weymouth. However, under nationalisation the Dorchester-
Weymouth line became part of the Southern Region.

In the old days, both the SR and the GWR had their own stations at
Dorchester. Today the SR station is 'Dorchester South' and the old
GWR station is 'Dorchester West'. Originally, the layout of the
Southern station was most unusual. The down platform, situated on the
curve leading round to the Great Western line, was set apart from the
up platform which was on a short spur, joined to the up main line by a
trailing connection. As a result, all up trains from Weymouth scheduled
to stop at Dorchester, had to run past the station and then set back into
the up platform.

195 *Above:* An LCGB special hauled by ex-LMS Stanier 'Black Five' No 45493
and 'West Country' Pacific No 34100 *Appledore*, setting off from Dorchester
West station for the run down to Weymouth.

After 'Dorchester West' became part of their region, the Southern Region
lost no time in replacing the GWR signals with their own type of upper
quadrant.

196 *Below:* Another enthusiasts' special, this time heading east from Dorchester
South station. The locomotive hauling the train is one of the excellent, and
highly individual Somerset & Dorset 7F 2-8-0s, No 53808. Happily, this engine
had been preserved and is at present being restored to running order by the
Somerset & Dorset Railway Museum Trust at Washford station on the West
Somerset Railway.

Bincombe Tunnels

These two tunnels come three miles south of Dorchester, at the top of the bank out of Weymouth. The main tunnel is just under half a mile long, whilst the much shorter one really serves no purpose other than to carry the line under the Dorchester–Weymouth road. Through both tunnels the line descends steeply at 1 in 52 towards Weymouth.

197 *Above:* The 3.35pm Bournemouth–Weymouth train, with 'West Country' Pacific No 34001 in charge, emerges from the southern end of the main tunnel on a June afternoon in 1967. By this time most of the Pacifics had had their nameplates removed prior to withdrawal, for steam was to end on the Southern Region in July 1967.

198 *Below:* One month earlier, on 9 May 1967, the same train, this time hauled by 'Merchant Navy' Pacific No 35030, drifts downhill out of the short tunnel.

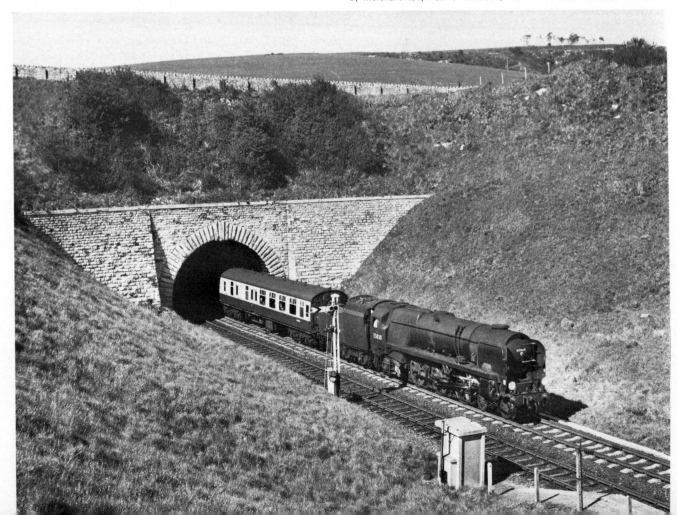

199 *Above:* In the late afternoon of a fine summer's day in June 1967, 'Merchant Navy' Pacific No 35023, hauling the 5.30pm Weymouth to Waterloo, bursts out of the short tunnel as she climbs strenuously uphill towards the main tunnel and Dorchester.

200 *Below:* Because of the severity of the bank out of Weymouth, most trains had an assisting engine up to Dorchester. One of the engines on banking duty on 20 July 1963, was BR 2-6-4T No 80081, seen here coasting downhill out of the short tunnel after assisting a train up to Dorchester. Smoke and fumes can be seen still pouring from the main tunnel mouth following the passage of the train up the bank some minutes earlier.

The Climb Out Of Weymouth

The four-mile climb out of Weymouth is very severe. Beginning at 1 in 187, this is followed by 1¼ miles of 1 in 74, which then steepens to 1 in 50 over the next 1¼ miles, and finally ends at 1 in 52 up through Bincombe Tunnel

201 *Above:* U class 2-6-0 No 31796 assists 'Merchant Navy' Pacific No 35023 *Holland-Afrika Line* up the bank with the 3.50pm Weymouth to Waterloo on 20 July 1963.

202 *Left:* BR Class 4 4-6-0 No 75065 climbing past Upwey Wishing Well Halt towards Bincombe Tunnel with the 11am (SO) Weymouth to Waterloo on an overcast Saturday in July 1963.

203 *Above:* Maximum effort! In difficult conditions, with squalls of rain driving across the open hillside, an unidentified 'West Country' Pacific, working very hard, struggles up the bank out of Weymouth with a heavy up Channel Islands boat train. She was receiving hearty rear-end assistance from a 2-6-4T, still hidden from view behind the trees in this picture.

204 *Below:* In sharp contrast BR Standard Class 5 4-6-0 No 73029, in charge of a light parcels train, came sailing up the bank in fine style on a lovely summer's evening in early May 1967.

Weymouth Quay

From Weymouth station, a line sets off to run for nearly a mile through the streets to the quay. All movements through the streets and along the quay are made with extreme caution, a flagman walking ahead of the train to warn road traffic. Steam engines working on the quay also carried a bell which was mounted on the left hand running plate just in front of the cab . . .

205 *Right:* Ex-Great Western pannier tank No 3737 eased her train of wagons carefully along the quay on a fine summer's afternoon in early May 1961 — a picture 'dated' by the two elderly Austin motorcars.

206 *Below:* . . . a little later in the afternoon (3.20pm according to the clock!) another ex-GWR pannier tank, No 1368 — this time one of the interesting, smaller variety with outside cylinders — came trundling along the quay, light engine.

207 *Above:* A train of perishables, just unloaded from a Channel Islands steamer, is hauled along the quay by ex-GWR pannier tank No 7780. Note the flagman walking ahead of the train. Before the introduction of 'double yellow lines', delays on the quay were often caused by thoughtless drivers parking their cars too close to the line. On some occasions, locked, unattended cars had to be manhandled out of the way!

The Portland Branch

208 *Below:* Until closure in 1965, a branch line used to diverge from the main line just before Weymouth station, to run down to Portland. Heading back through the rain from Portland towards Weymouth on 25 August 1963, is the Southern Counties Touring Society's excursion, hauled by an ex-Great Western pannier tank. (See Plates 96 and 181.)

Weymouth Motive Power Depôt

209 *Above:* A general view of the Running Shed on 7 May 1961. The two engines in the foreground are an ex-Great Western 'Modified Hall', No 6968 *Woodcock Hall*, and SR Pacific No 34090 *Sir Eustace Missenden*.

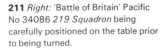

210 *Left:* The Weymouth shedmaster, Charles Attwell, (on the right) chatting to Harold Morris, the Bath shedmaster who accompanied me on my expedition to Weymouth on Sunday 7 May 1961. Charles Attwell is now Area Manager, Barnham. Harold Morris, the last shedmaster at Bath, Green Park, retired in 1966 and died 11 years later in 1977. His passing brought sadness to many members of the railway enthusiast fraternity to whom he had always been a very good friend.

211 *Right:* 'Battle of Britain' Pacific No 34086 *219 Squadron* being carefully positioned on the table prior to being turned.